THE GRAVEYARDS ARE FULL

A POETIC DEDICATION TO ALL VICTIMS OF GENGER-BASED VIOLENCE

BY

MOSA SEKELE MASHITISHO

The Graveyards are Full
A poetic dedication to all victims of Gender-Based Violence

Published by Mosa Sekele Mashitisho

Pretoria West, 0183

mosasekele@gmail.com

ISBN 978-0-6397-9336-8

eISBN 978-0-6397-9337-5

2 4 6 8 10 9 7 5 3 1

Layout and cover design by Boutique Books

Printed in South Africa

Contents

<u>Preface</u>

This book is a poetic dedication to all the victims of gender-based violence. It is written with love for the ones who have fallen prey to this scourge. It is also written to evoke empathy, to heal and to offer hope to everyone that we can still heal our nation by opening lines of communication through books, songs, support groups, media and many other ways.

We need more education about how people should communicate their emotions and feelings openly, so that we minimise these feelings of being unheard, misunderstood, angry and insecure.

Growing up exposed to situations of GBV at a very young age but not really hearing of change stories, we yearn for men who are willing to stand up and say this is the monster I used to be and now I am dedicated to protecting and loving our women. This is said not forgetting that there are, even though not nearly as many and often unspoken about, men who also suffer gender-based violence at the hands of their female partners. We hope that one day they will gather the strength to speak up, to fight and to eventually leave before being deprived of the chance to live.

We are no longer in a space where we need to educate victims on how to protect themselves, but rather we need men who are willing to be leaders, protectors and mostly lovers, instead of killers. We need women who will take back their roles as nurturers, incubators and healers and change the narrative. If we all take a moment to reflect, we will realise that our differences don't make us ugly or bad or even insufficient beings, but rather beautiful people who combine to create new and exciting stories and, once we appreciate each other's uniqueness, we will all see that **our stories are beautiful.**

Man, I feel your pain. It was not your fault.
Woman, I feel your pain. It was not your fault either.
Let us heal together. Let us be beautiful together.

Love, Mosa M.

The graveyards are full

The graveyards are full of women once loved.
Women once told how beautiful and worthy of love they were.
The graveyards are full of women once promised for better or
  worse.
To love and to hold, to cherish and to care,
And yet they carry six feet of soil upon their chests.
Oh, what shame!
For all this began in the name of love.

The graveyards are full of women who were told to be strong,
Who were told that it was okay to endure pain.
Bathi emendweni kuya bekezelwa.
Women are told "*lebitla la mosadi ke bogadi*",
Told that they will die in their marital homes.
We thought this was a figurative speech that
Told women that they would now carry their husband's last
  name.
But this has become a literal statement
That says that women get married to get murdered.
Given beautiful send offs with wedding ceremonies,
While carrying a kist as a reminder that death awaits them in
  the name of love.
What a punishment, disguised in sweet memories.

The graveyards are full of women who were told not to have
  an opinion,
Taught to stick it out for the sake of the kids
And reserve their right to show emotions of anger and hurt
Because the man would feel undermined

And end up beating her up and thereafter blame her for
    making him do it.
The graveyards are full of women who died at the mercy of a
    man.
Full of women covered in makeup to disguise black eyes and
    bruises
For fear of being judged and laughed at by society.
Because the man said "*bazothini*" about him.
Strong, courageous, loving and caring women are no more,
Their warmth has been frozen six feet under.
Their smiles have been wiped away by rivers of their
    children's tears.
Oh, the poor orphans, growing up in the most hurtful
    environments,
Where a man can punch a woman in the face and kick her in
    the stomach
Only because she saw a fault in him.
Only because she was not humble enough.
And just! Just because his ego would not let him apologise,
For he would feel weak and naked in the eyes of his sick peers
Who call him "*skhokho*" for not being controlled by a woman.

The graveyards are full, but I still hear screams.
I hear the screams of a woman being raped,
They say because her dress was too short and tempting and
Because he could not hold himself back when he saw those
    thighs calling to him.
As he pulls her into the dirty passage by the dump site,
I see her kicking and fighting until her last breath.
She is no more because she was too hot.
I hear screams of a lesbian woman down the road,

As she pleads with the group of young men,
Dropouts even, who could not care to be educated
But thought they needed to "correct" her corrupted mindset of
    loving women
And remind her of her sexual duties as a woman.
I hear her pleading with them not to hurt her,
Until they kill her because she recognised one of them.
I hear the screams of a housewife,
As he stabs her powerless body with the beer bottle he just
    emptied into his stomach.
Only because she asked where he slept last night,
Only to come wanting food at four in the morning –
Food she did not cook because he did not buy any.
She could not afford to buy any because he forbade her from
    working,
And yet compared her to working class ladies and called her
    lazy.
I hear the screams of a young, independent woman
Who was hijacked and murdered by associates
For landing a promotion at work without having to give sexual
    favours.
They said she was too arrogant and they had to teach her a
    lesson.
Unfortunately, she never graduated from the lesson:
The position and the power went to her head,
And that is what killed her, they said.

Land that was supposed to host beautiful family homes
Has been cleared to make space for new graves;
To make space for dead women.

The graveyards are full
Of women who are said to be stubborn and not submissive
   enough.
Of women who are denied the right to speak up,
The right to be outspoken and free-spirited.
They say women must submit or die.
But to where do we submit when there is no address?
Women are told to listen to the man when he speaks,
Never to correct him or suffer the axe, the rape, the knife, and
   the gun.
To follow him, even when he has no idea of where he is going.
To never ask him anything but to follow and submit to him.
But I ask again: to where do we submit when there is no
   address?

I am Leaving

I am leaving.
I am leaving because I want to live.
I am leaving because I want to raise our children.
I want to see them grow.
I want to see them become better people.
I want to see them explore love and find its true meaning and
    joy.
I want to see them make mistakes
So that I can correct them and help draw lessons from them.
I am leaving, not because I do not love you anymore;
I am leaving because the love has become dangerous.
I am leaving, not to punish you,
But to free you from these poisonous bonds
Of the monster growing inside of you,
Surrounding and engraving your whole being.
Consuming you into total monstrosity.
I am leaving for the freedom of you not going to jail because of
    me.
I am leaving to avoid taking the blame from your family,
For turning you into a monster they never knew before I came.
For turning you into a monster you didn't want to become.
I am leaving for my life to be spared.
I am leaving because I have run out of tears.
I am leaving because I still want to live.
Yes! I repeat that I am leaving you because I want to stay alive.
Because I want to raise our children
And to let them know that it's okay to choose life over abuse.
I want them to know that love does not have to carry pain,

To know that love does not have to hurt and that it is a
    beautiful feeling
And that, even when it has ripened, it does not have to expire.
I want them to know that love is fun.
In my departure, I hope you use this space to get help.
I hope you find peace and heal from yourself
Because you have become a deadly disease.
I hope that hate will not consume you.
I hope that you forgive yourself because you need that.
And I really hope you will not hate me for leaving
But that you will understand why I could not stay anymore.

A Woman's Love Suffers Longer

A woman's love suffers longer.
You hurt me and I cried.
You see, you mistakenly took my tears for weakness.
I did not cry because you hurt me, nor because I was weak.
I also did not cry to get your sympathy because that I do not
    need –
And I know that if I did, I would not get it anyway.
I cried because I thought of you and tried to justify your
    wrongs for you.
I tried to understand that you were hurting too.
That you could not manage your pain other than by shoving it
    down my throat.
Unfortunately, it went straight to the heart.
I did not cry because you defeated me and won the argument,
Nor because I lacked the will to reciprocate.
Believe me when I say I could do more to you;
Much more than you actually did to me.
But then I would fall into the same ditch that you fell into.
I cried because I thought of your hurt more than mine.
I still have tears in my eyes,
Wondering if you have thought of your deed or healed from it.
Wondering if hurting me has lessened your own burden.
Hoping that, from the corner at which you stand peeping,
You do not feel any sense of triumph but rather you introspect
And ask why I never sought revenge when it was due to me.

But in case you don't ask...
Just in case you never wonder...
I did not cry from a point of weakness

But from the strength I possess.
Strength that easily narrates to me the story of your pain.
Strength that forced me out of self-pity so I could empathise
    with your situation.
I cried, looking at how deep your pain is.
It is so deep that you have accepted it as a norm and
    internalised the pain.
You have made it your story so that, even when you hurt me,
You mistake my pain for some sort of weakness.
I still have tears in my eyes,
Hoping that you have healed.
But in case you're still watching from that corner,
Hoping for my retaliation or even my fall,
I want you to know that love suffers longer.
My heart is made that way.
A woman's love will suffer first.
It will seek to cure your pain before the pain you inflict on her.
Before licking its own wounds, it licks yours with care.
So, when you hurt me and expected to see my reaction,
I cried because your pain weighed on me.
You tried to make me feel worthless.
Fortunately, I never placed my worth in your careless hands.
I chose to value myself, despite your ill opinions of me,
And refused to be limited by you.
I let love win and kept my side of humanity.
So, in case you wonder why I still have not hurt you back,
Just know that my love for you chose to understand.
Just know that a woman's love suffers longer.

CHRONICLES OF THE WOMB BEARER

Cursed from conception,
I carry the burden of pain and tears.
As a young child, I was raped and molested;
As a young woman, I was beaten and bruised;
And as a young mother, I was mercilessly murdered,
Leaving my daughter to suffer the same fate.
The say we give life while ours is taken ruthlessly away from
  us.
Whose tears will it take to save us and hear our cry?
Who is that kind-hearted gentleman,
Who will come and love us full circle?
Without conditions and without terms.
Who is that gentle man whose true character is written on his
  forehead,
That we may run to him for safety?
Have we not died enough to spare the remaining ones?
Is it not bad enough that we suffer period pains when we do
  not conceive
And suffer labour pains when we do bring life?
Then, due to complications, our tummies are cut to deliver this
  life,
And our scars remain a curse to our appeal in your eyes.
Is it not enough that you still want to kill us?
We are still slapped, kicked and punched.
We are still stabbed, and mutilated, and hung on trees and
  poles.
We are still thrown in dumps and pits,
Buried without our families knowing where.
A woman in our time lives in fear of her loved one.

Does I love you not mean anything anymore?
Has your love for us reached its expiry date?
Or are these just chronicles of the womb bearer?
For how long must we keep empowering victims
Teaching them to stay safe and alert?
What kind of life is this?
For how long must we teach women to defend themselves,
When we should be acknowledging where the problems lies
    and fixing that.
We are tired!
We are dying!
These are screams from the tombs.
These are cries of restless spirits seeking peace and fearful
    souls begging for life.
These are cries of restless mothers and daughters and sisters
    and grandmothers
Fearing and asking for their lives to be spared.
Our wombs are not breeding grounds for murderers
That we should curse the ones that bore these monsters.
Our wombs are a blessing from God to create life safely, with
    warmth and care.
Our wombs are a symbol of God's love for humanity.
For a child to come from a place of pure love,
A safe haven until they are ready to be born into this world.
Our wombs are not an institution of brutality and extreme
    hate.
Our wombs are cubbyholes for life to form beautifully, calmly
    and steadily
At God's pace and intention for beauty in creation.
Can you not appreciate that much and let us be?
Chronicles of the womb bearer

Cursed from the womb!
Last seen in the tomb!
Bruised and battered!
A woman's body has suffered.
Could she rest in peace?
Could her soul rest with ease?

I WISH I HAD a WOMB

Dear Wife,
I wish I had a womb like you.
So, I could carry the lives of our kids, which you have
    mercilessly aborted.
I wish I had a womb to carry my name forever.
To keep my pride as a man and as a father.
I have tried to endure childlessness and continued loving you,
Even in times when you made it hard to;
To love you even in times where you were not worthy of my
    love.
I have tried to justify your abuse for hormonal imbalances.
Little did I know it came from the multiple abortions
When you told me you had miscarriages.
I tried to endure the emotional blackmail,
The mental, emotional and even physical abuse.
I tried to justify all that manipulation just so I could be a better
    man.
But I guess the hate in you grew further until you eventually
    burst and confessed
To squeezing the life out of our children.
Could you not have just left me if there was no love?
Could you not have just told me I was not worthy to father
    your children?
Instead of the hate, the abuse and all the murders of my kids?
Oh, my dear wife,
I wish I had a womb like you
Because my mother, who carried me in her womb,
Told me that blessed is she that has a womb
For she has the favour of the Lord to carry life

And deliver God's intention for creation into the world.
Blessed is the woman who has done the Lord's work honestly
    and lovingly so.
I mean not to curse you, my dear wife, but I cry for my lost
    children.
Ones I could have loved and cared for, God willing,
But I guess you had the deciding advantage.
I wish I had a womb so I could carry my kids
Since they were too heavy for you.
And this is why I must leave you and find someone
Who will carry the remaining ones
Because, as much as I cannot carry children, believe you me I
    can nurture them.
So, for you and me, my beloved wife, this is goodbye.

Give men flowers

I weep for my brothers
Whose hearts are hard as rocks,
Yet they feel broken inside.
I weep for my brothers
Whose silent tears have now filled the rivers,
Yet they still soldier on like men.
Cheeks dug like furrows,
They still draw smiles like clowns.
Tired as they are, boots torn as they are,
They still soldier on, like good men should.

I weep for the brother next door,
Whose father calls him weak because he does not contribute a
    cent to the house.
His father worships the ground which the little brother walks
    on,
Because fortunately he has life figured out at twenty-six.
My brother next door has no say in what they watch on
    television
Because he does not know how much the monthly
    subscription is,
Nor can he decide that he's tired of chicken
When he cannot even afford a tin of fish.

I weep for my brother across the road
Whose wife beats him to a pulp,
But he cannot go to the police station
Because what man does that?
Which man can admit he's being abused

In a society that would mock his masculinity?
Police would laugh and tell him to man up.
Family says he's been fed a love portion.
Friends call him a snot face.
Girls call him a sissy boy and a mama's boy.

I weep for my brother at mam Aggie's house,
Who lives life in secret because no one can know he is gay.
Because God forbid his father should know:
He would crucify him without hesitation.
What will the other pastors say?
The congregation will question his ability to lead.
What will they say about his failure
To control his household
While claiming to run the house of the Lord?
What a contradiction; what a joke!
He lives in the shadows of what a man is supposed to be
While forcing himself to be with a woman he feels nothing for,
Just so his mother can boast to the stokvel ladies
About how perfect her son is.

I weep for my brother in the village,
Who left school in Grade Nine
To go be a herder for the chief,
Just so his sickly mother and siblings
Could go to bed with a full stomach.
While his mates boasted about solve for x,
He could not even count how many sheep went missing
And he did not get his wage on that Friday.

I weep for his yearning and desperation to see his child,
But he is denied because he is not enough
So he has to watch his son grow
In the hands of another reckless and abusive man.

I weep for my learned brother in Alexandra,
Who works a high paying job
But cannot even afford a pair of shoes for himself
Because he has to take his mother out of the slums
And build her a mansion in the far east.
He has to pay his brother's school fees,
His older sister's expensive lifestyle,
While putting her kids through crèche.
Each time he wants to live his life,
He gets reminded of how selfish he is,
How his mom went through two days of labour
To bring him to earth,
And how his useless father just upped and left.
He pays for his father's sins and his mother's wrong choice in
     men.
What a shame!

I weep for my brother who lives with his stepfather.
One who has been molesting him for the past seven years
But he could not say anything at all
Because it would end his mother's marriage.
I see how she pretends not to know
While it also eats her up like a ghost
Lurking in the darkness, waiting for prey.
I see the anger boiling up in him

And each time he reacts they say he is a rebel of an ungrateful
    son
Who does not appreciate the efforts of the stepfather,
Who took him as his own.
Little do they know that indeed,
He has taken him on as his own sex toy.

I weep for my brother at the back opposite house,
Who has been raising three kids for nine years
Thinking they were his seed.
I remember how the birthday parties were spoken about for
    months, even after they passed,
Because he made sure to create the best memories for his
    children.
Only to find out they were his brother's own.
As he remembers how people used to say,
"They look like your brother,"
And he would say to them, "My brother and I look like twins".
Little did he know...

I weep for my brothers!
I weep for the silent cries they cannot hold anymore.
Help! Help the boy child. Help the man!
Allow him to speak out.
Allow him to be heard, to be seen!
Nurture him into the greatness he's meant to get to.
Talk him out of his suicidal thoughts.
Pull him out of his depression.
Give him flowers; give them flowers!
Give men flowers:
They deserve them too.

Tell them we love them.
Tell them they are enough.
Tell them it's okay to hurt.
Tell them to talk about it.
Tell them to cry and hug them.
Please, yes! Tell men it's okay to cry.
Tell the big men with muscles
That it's okay to cry.
Allow them to weep for themselves
And give them safe spaces to heal.
And on their journey to healing, give them flowers.
Give men flowers!

As good as pulling the trigger

Confessions of a guilty wife.
He asked me to be kind with my words,
And believe me, I was giving it to him.
Telling him about that village witch he calls Mother,
And that useless man he calls Father,
Who did nothing good for them.
Just as he (my husband) did nothing for us.
I told him how I was tired of feeding his lazy self
And how he could go hang himself, for all I cared.

He asked me to be kind with my words.
And believe me, I was sky high,
Soaring with anger and saying it all,
While looking down on this poor man
Who gave his all for me to be where I was.
Mighty and successful.
A boss babe and independent supermom.
When he asked me to tone it down, for the kids not to hear,
I asked him if he knew those kids.
Hell, I asked him if he knew how kids were made.
And only then did he realise that they were not his.

I poured on him so hard,
Like the heavy rains before the winter.
I made sure I sent shivering chills to his spine.
I was fed up and I did not realise how it all went to his heart.
Never mind that his mind was long destroyed
So much so that he had no chance to think anything right
Other than my daily gentle reminder

That he was not man enough to handle me.
I reminded him of his empty promises
That he said were soon to materialise but never did.
I forgot how he sacrificed them and funded my hustle
When no one else but him believed in me.
I reminded him about his successful friends who laughed at
    him behind his back.
Real men who knew what they wanted in life.

I am not proud of the things I said to him
But I was fed up with him.
And now I am too late.
He is gone. He took his life.
In my defence, he was selfish.
He has left me to raise the children alone.
I forgot that I indirectly told him they were not his.
He decided life was not worth it anymore.
He'd lost his wife and what he thought were his children.
He'd lost the only things that motivated him to go on every day
And he was not doing badly at all, just not better than me.

What will I tell his family?
They knew him as a happy man.
They never knew about his marital problems.
He never told them about our fights,
Or should I say my abusive behaviour towards him?
They thought he had the best life and wife.
Yet all my friends heard me rave
About his family's generational curses and failures.
They knew about my plans to divorce him and find a worthy
    man.

One who would treat me like the princess I am... was.
All that is gone now.
I am left an empty shell with regrets.
I am left a guilty wife.

He left me a note.
He titled it, "As good as pulling the trigger".
It was a public letter that he dedicated to me,
Line by line, reading it in a video he posted online for all to see.
He also posted a video of me going at him like a mad woman.
On the day he asked me to be kind with my words,
He posted it online, just before he pulled the trigger.
I found out from other people, as I cared little for his social
    pages.
I found out from other people
That my beloved husband was no more.
And, before feeling the pain,
I had to feel the shame of being a useless wife.
I had to feel the guilt of being a cruel wife.
I also had to face this judgemental society.

How can I apologise to him? To the world?
Without it seeming like the rehearsed performance
Of a not so sorry wife.
I really am sorry, but it will not count for anything now
For everyone knows what was in my heart,
How I wished the worst upon my husband's life, unashamedly.
Everyone heard when he begged me,
When he asked me to be kind with my words,
And I said he should go beg in the streets.
Maybe then he would have gotten something out of life.

So, he went on and begged on the highway to heaven,
And he got his immediate response – the heavens welcomed
    him.

Am I left a widow?
Or am I left a shell of a guilty wife?
Whose words were as good as pulling the trigger.
I have killed my husband with my words
And sorry will never be enough.
I may weep, but no one will feel for me
Because, at the end of the day, I caused his death.
He asked me to be kind with my words
But they were just too sharp.
They were just as good as pulling the trigger.

Farewell, my Queen

Farewell, my queen.
If only I could see through her smile.
The hurt and the loneliness she felt.
If I could hear the burdened silent cries
Beyond the cracked voice that said
I am okay, it is okay.
If I could feel the shivering chills she had when I came closer.
When she apologised, even when I was the one in the wrong.
Maybe then I would recognise the monster in me.
No, I am not asking you to understand
Nor believe that I did not know better.
It is just that she took it so well that
I too thought all was well.
I thought she was a strong woman
Because always when I wronged her
She forgave me, one more time.
The monster in me told me that if she took it twice,
And much more than that,
Then it was okay for me to make it a habit.
The monster in me convinced me
That not hitting her meant I was not abusive.
All the belittling and swearing,
The blackmail and the manipulation,
All of it fed my ego, saying, "I am a man".
And her saying it was okay told me she was okay.
All of it made me think she was okay.
Little did I know that she was a walking dead.
She was broken and empty and depressed.
Little did I know that she was leaving me soon.

Her heart and soul had already left.
She had already shut the door.
All that was left was an empty shell.

If only I could say that I am sorry.
If I could listen to her one more time,
But this time pay attention to her broken voice.
Feel the emptiness of her shallow heart that I drained out.
And fill it with the love I promised her.
If only I could have been there, just a second before she killed
   herself.
But even the wisest of men can never reverse time.
Last Wednesday, I put flowers beside her hospital bed.
I said a little prayer that the Lord would keep her for me.
I prayed that she survived and woke up.
But I was too late, and the Lord kept her for Himself.
And when the doctor murmured, I am sorry,
I knew I was too late: she was gone.
I knew the monster in me had eaten her.
Today I am here, praying for my healing,
Not only to survive life without her
But that, for her, I could change and never feed my monster
   self.
I pray that, for her, I never lay my hand on anyone
And I never kill someone else with my words.

Today I pray that my fellow brothers learn from my mistake
And cherish the only visible blessing the Lord gives to us,
For even the most dignified funeral
Does not erase the deeds of unkindness.
It does not and can never bring back what I had.

You! That remain blessed,
Appreciate the scent of your flowers while they still flourish.
Because when they are dead, and the stench of the
    surrounding carcass rises,
All you can ever hope for is but a memory:
A memory of a life you had the chance to live but never did
And instead squeezed out the life of the one that gave you
    yours.
To everyone that remains, I am deeply sorry.
I am sorry that she died in my care.
To my one true love, I am sorry.
I am sorry that I broke you.
Farewell, my queen.

WHen THe CReDITS ROLL...

When the credits roll...
When the story of my life ends,
When God the Director says, "It is a wrap".
When He says cut!
It is done, she is no more,
What will be said of me?
What will the story of my life be?
Or will it be the story of my death that prevails?
Will I be trending on the hash tags?
Will there be T-shirts worn with my face on them
And a full coverage of my funeral on the news?

When the credits roll...
Will it be a standing ovation for me?
Will my strength be commemorated or mocked?
Will my Maker accept my bruised body?
Will I not be crucified for staying in hell?
Or will those who were slain before me,
Gracefully welcome one more of their own?
Will they feel I could have fought more?
Will my kids whom I leave behind
Know that I stayed and endured for them?

When the credits roll...
Will the villain finally be happy?
Will the thirst finally be quenched?
Will I have paid it forward for all?
Or will it just be one more?
Will it be the last episode of the first season in a series?

Or the end of a tragic movie with a planned sequel.
Will I still qualify as a protagonist?
I did hear they do not die
But I learned each story has its own line.

When the credits roll, and I am no more…
Will they remember when I was denied help and told to
    endure?
Will they still feel proud of me for my strength and forgiving
    spirit?
Will they say, "She was strong"?
Or will they change and say, she could have left?
When he finds and reads my diary, will he show them, or will
    he burn it?
For fear of identifying the monster he is between the lines.
Will he even be at my funeral, or will he be in a jail cell?
Will he be sorry, or not?
Will he explain to them and to our kids?

When the credits roll, and I am no more…
When the last scene shuts black,
Each one looking to see their names going up,
Each one reminiscing their role,
Will they be proud of the montage in their minds?
Will they be happy with their performances?
Will they then expect awards?
Or will there be casualties of regret, as in war?
Will it be "what ifs" and "had it not beens"?
What will the cast and crew say when my Maker says cut?

When the credits roll, and I am no more...
I pray there will not be a march in my name.
I pray my face will not be flying on placards.
I pay there would not be a #justice_for_her trending.
I implore you not to say, "We could have".
I pray you feel no regret for ignoring my cries, now when I
    need you.
I pray you all do not plead guilty for being bystanders.
I pray his family will finally see the truth.
I pray my family will forgive, as they always told me to.
I pray he forgives himself and changes.

When the credits roll, and I am no more...
Will they remember my story through my life or my tragic
    death?
Will they remember my bruises or my bubbliness?
Will they remember my blue eyes or blue eyeshadow?
Will they remember my broken ribs or my figure belt?
Or will everyone remember the beauty
Of the flowers he put by my hospital bedside,
Or these fresh ones laid on my tomb?
Will the scent of those flowers even be of my favourite
    perfume?

When the credits roll... Will you remember the screams?

Red Flags

Red flags...
Love is not blind.
I saw everything and I still stayed.
I saw the text messages and the call histories.
I saw when she told him she was leaving him
And he asked for one more month to divorce me.
I saw the flowers besides my bed at the hospital,
After he had beaten me to a pulp yester-night.
I saw the love letters and promises that
Quoted I am sorry, I love you, I did not mean to,
As I lay helplessly on the hospital bed,
Afraid to even call my mother and aunts
Because they said in this chapter of life we endure.
I saw the not-so-sorry face.
When he said to my face that I pushed him too hard.
And it was my attitude that drove his anger.

I saw all the red flags and I still stayed.
I stayed and endured the ill treatment,
All in the name of love is blind.
I dare you not to say that one more time.
Unless you want to follow me
To where we go but never come back.
Love is not blind, so I dare you not to say that.
Love is not a fist that seeks to punch.
It is not a boot that seeks to kick down.
It is not pain that seeks to hurt.

I saw the red flags and still I stayed.
I hoped he would change, but he became worse.
He worked on my insecurities
And made me feel like I deserved the blame.
I stayed because I thought I had to,
That it was part of the deal that marriage is.
I thought he was building my character, as he often said.
I saw the red flags and still I stayed on,
Sighing when his family admired my strength
And thereby thinking I was an example
To one little girl facing the same route.
I thought I taught her to endure and stick it out,
For the sake of family –
For the sake of love and our vows –
And not being the one blamed for initiating the sin called
    divorce.

I saw the red flags and still I stayed.
And today it can only be taught in social circles
That I should have left.
It will be taught that it is okay to leave.
So, I dare you not to say love is blind.
Even when the red flags are blowing in your face,
I dare you not to say that love is blind
Because I saw the red flags, and still I stayed...

One day I will be independent of your love

One day I will be independent of your love.
I will know that only I can love me truly and unconditionally.
One day I will be content with just me
And forget about the perfect picture of us
That only exists in my imaginary wish list.
I will forget about how far we have come
And remember that you have continued without me.
I will remember who I was before you came into the picture,
Even though I have framed a whole lot of us
On the walls of my heart.
I will forget that you once promised me heaven and earth
And naively I believed you,
Even though you did not offer a star to begin with.
Yes, I fell for the words and fell deeply, blindly and passionately
    in love,
But along the way I rose up and out of love with the image of
    me without you.
I forgot the beauty that lies in my spirit
And how honest my love for you is.
I focused on how I see you loving me away
And forging your life next to me while I watch in disbelief
How we have grown apart, yet I still stand where we started,
Blindly and hopelessly wishing that it is a dream
And, when I wake up, you will still be smiling at me,
Like I am your world, little as I am.
You once convinced me that
I filled a huge space in your heart.
Yet today, here I am...
Lost next to you, watching you live away your life,

Happy without me.
Waking up next to you every morning
With the hope for a good morning kiss on the forehead;
Yet receiving a cold, emotionless look has become our truth.
I can only remember
That I was once loved and that is all that it is.
A beautiful memory in my mind
That I am yet to let go of as I try to forge my life
Without hearing you say, "I love you," again.
But I should say to myself that I love me.
One day I will be independent of your love
And finally love me once more.

To see you Love me now

Dear Wife...
Mother of my unborn babies.
Bearer of my unachieved goals.
Reminder of my promises not kept.
Planner of my unattended aspirations.
Oh, how it hurts... to see you love me now.
To witness you wanting me so badly.
To see you needing me so desperately.
Looking at you, I see a woman I once loved.
A future I once wished for and vowed to work hard for.
Believe you me, I did work hard for you.
Looking at you, I see vows, prayers, promises.
I see brokenness and shattered dreams of a hopeful soul.

Should I blame myself for loving you unconditionally?
For seeming desperate for your attention?
My mind takes me back to happier times.
To the love that was once painted in your eyes.
I remember when I used to eat and breathe your love.
Oh, maybe that too was what I wanted to believe.
I remember how beautiful you looked and felt for me in my
thoughts.
I still hear your mother's words and your grandmother's
advisory reprimands.
I hear my mother and her sisters' ululations.
From that day you were finally mine and mine alone.
Your uncles said they were happy with the number of cows we
sent.
I remember that smile on my face when you were finally mine.

Oh, my dear wife, to see you love me now,
After you left me for dead
Not even with the slightest care, fright or flinch.
As you closed the door to our promises and vows
And you closed the story of our book.
Even when I, with the last of my strength shouted, "I still love
    you,"
You still left. You left me.
You said it was not your responsibility to care for an addict.
Yes. It was not your fault that I ended up an addict,
But it was your vow that for better or worse you would stay –
    yet you did not.
You knew how those power-hungry hypocrites robbed us of
    our success.
You saw how it destroyed me, yet you still left.
Yes. It was not your fault that I soaked myself in alcohol
And I suffocated myself in the stench of drugs and weed.
I could have done better, but my generation said men don't cry.
Perhaps if I had cried you would have felt my pain,
But it was too much of a shame...

My generation taught me that I had to carry the iron rod, even
    when it burnt my back.
It said "*Monna ke nku o llela teng*": a man suffers in silence.
But my silence was too loud, and my sober mind could not
    take it anymore.
Hence, I drugged my mind in an attempt to numb the pain.
In all of that, I needed you and you were not there.
Even seated right next to me you were very far away:
With your thoughts, your body and your companionship, you
    were just far away.

I remember how you would wear your best dress and make
   up,
And one by one they fetched you, right at the gate of our home.
One by one, having their best nights with my beloved wife.
You were beautiful then; no man could refuse your charm.
You were a damsel in distress and all knights in shining
   armour were ready to rescue you,
To save you from the sham of a marriage you were in and an
   excuse for a husband you had.
They were all ready to give you a better life.
Maybe, if you'd just picked one you would have gotten it. Who
   knows?
My poor, loving mother took me back and rebuilt me. Like only
   a mother could.
May her soul rest in peace. She was proud of me when she
   died.
She was happy that she'd healed me.
She was proud that I was more successful than I was before.
She rebuilt me, like only a mother would.
Something you may never know, even given three lifetimes.
Because you took a decision alone.
To tie your fallopian tubes without me knowing.
Without asking me if I would like to be a father or not.
A blessing in disguise. What would our children have
   witnessed?

To see you love me now hurts, my dearest wife.
You loved the good times
And they always reciprocated the love.
Perhaps you were a vibe magnet.
Because fun used to follow you everywhere.

You even gave up our chance to be parents
Because you needed to maintain your figure. I see it's still
    there.
I see you are still beautiful.
But I remember you once told me that one cannot eat one's
    beauty.

I have gotten better. I have spoken to women, nurturers,
And they gave me permission to cry.
They said I should tell my brothers too that they should cry.
So, they let me cry and, when I had had enough…
They reminded me that I had to dust off the pain and start
    over.
And so I did. But not with just work and other stuff;
I started over with someone else.
I found a new love. One who worked with my mother to pick
    me up.
One who moulded me into a new man. A beautiful man. A
    beautiful story.
By beautiful, I don't mean my looks, although I am quite
    handsome.
I am beautiful – body, mind and soul… And so is my wife.
The mother of my kids.
Oh, I didn't say! We have three now.
Dear Wife, or should I say, dear Judy.
To see you love me now makes me feel sorry for you.
Because that factory burned.
And evidence has shown that
You had the petrol bottle and fire-lighters.
Footage has you starting the fire.
Now, how dare you want to claim the ashes!

Life as we know it

Life, and the choices it affords us. Here is a collection of words known to me and you through our day-to-day experiences in life. We are confronted by many challenges, opportunities, and many other encounters.

We experience joy, sadness, hurt, pain, healing, miracles and pure bliss, and that is just life as we know it.

We meet different people in our distinct stages of our lives and each one of them leaves a mark on our lives that is either a curse and burden, or a blessing. We are privileged with the blessing of choice to choose which one of these we want to nurture in the story of our life – and that is just the beauty of it all... choice. We all want to be happy, but different life circumstances almost always push us in a different direction and the choice to be strong and willing to keep on keeping on is our greatest weapon.

When in dark moments in our lives, we often feel like we are being punished or we are cursed, but we have a choice to motivate ourselves and our loved ones to do better, no matter what we are faced with and that again is life as we know it.

When I First Died

The sound of silence so loud in my head.
The darkness of a night that held me captive.
The pounding rhythm of fear in my heart.
I was a prisoner of that heart-wrenching darkness.
I was kept far away from myself.
As I stood there, looking at my soul-deprived self
I was walking in that dark cave,
Falling into holes and hitting myself against the walls.
Who knows if I was walking in circles?
Going past the same spot, again and again.
As I was walking without knowing where I was headed,
There sounded a multitude of voices singing from a distance.
Though I could not make sense of what was said,
It sounded like a harmonious song
And my heart yearned to get there.
It pleaded with my feet to fight for their depleted strength
To carry me through to the other side,
For it knew that was where the awakening of my soul dwelled.
And so, my feet, crippled as they felt,
Carried me to the place I so desperately hoped to be at.
As I walked, hoping to get closer to the sound of voices,
It kept moving away from me.
It seemed to be going further away by each verse.
I started forcing my feet to run.
Despair and fear made me weaker,
But longing and yearning for salvation
Made me forget about the horns and thorns
That mercilessly prickled my feet
And scratched my body.

I was running against time.
I could feel the warm blood oozing from my body
As it went cold and dried on my skin,
And spilled on the ground as though traces of a map showing
    direction.
I could hear as my blood fell into the river that passed through
    the dark tunnel,
One drop after the other, like rain drops from tree leaves
After the storm has passed. And the winds that howled
Gave me cold shivers that went deep to my damp soul.
I was tired of running and, as I stood there panting,
Desperately grasping what air I could breathe,
I Suddenly heard a mighty voice
Shouting so loudly that it echoed a few times.
"Stop!" it said with a deep note.
"Stop and look up to your Saviour."
Out of fear of whatever it may have been,
I stopped and looked up and around.
I started running again when I saw nothing.
"Stop, I say to you!"
The voice reprimanded hastily and so I stopped, still panting.
I looked up, almost hesitantly with grave fear.
Then that song started again.
It sounded more joyous, more confident, more content.
And beyond the pain, beyond the powerlessness,
Beyond the darkness,
I saw a beam of light that came with a bit of warmth.
It was like a mountain had been shifted out of my way.
The voice asked me,
Do you believe? Even if it is a drop in the ocean.
I nodded a desperate yes,

Almost invisible and shy to show.
"Go in then," said the voice to me.
The door opened wide as I walked forward
And I saw an angel in my image.
She smiled and said to me, "Welcome home, come inside".
She held my hand and hugged me.
She walked with me and showed me to everyone
And then came straight to me and entered my body.
She and I became one and I felt whole, alive and content.
They showed me the promise that I wrote to myself.
A promise I'd made in my school uniform.
They showed me what I still had to do.
They showed me a grand opening to my play.
They showed me that, when I first died, I could not rest in
    peace.

On the window sill

I always sat there,
By the window in my room.
Every morning, noon and afternoon
I watched, as little boys and girls
Were rushed to respective preschools.
I looked at the new graders,
In their cute new uniforms, waving to moms and dads,
And the smiles of pride on their mothers' and fathers' faces,
Happy, emotional tears drawing on their cheeks,
With pride reigning in their hearts.
I watched teens going to their first day of high school,
Some extremely nervous and some very joyous,
All hopeful for a bright future ahead.
I looked at how they built friendships
And how they easily picked fights in the streets.
As they grew past adolescence,
I watched as they celebrated their matric results and started
    varsity life,
Free of their parents' rules.
I watched them focus on their studies,
Striving with clear views of what they wanted their future to
    be like.
I watched them graduate.
With a glimpse of envy, and pride too.
I watched them make better career choices in life.
I saw them achieve their goals and dreams.
I saw them post, "Mama, I made it,"
And the priceless looks on their parents' faces, which shone
    with

Joy.
The pride was too much to contain.
And then I looked at my own,
Still praying for my goals.
For the dreams I once shared with them.
I saw their stubborn hope disappear.
Their longing and wishing fade into despair,
Finally giving in to a future lost to procrastinations
Because I sat there every morning and watched life pass me by.
Busy over-thinking and over-analysing.
They say the bigger the dream,
The scarier it becomes;
And the more it scares you, the more
You know it is the one for you.
It is the one that is shouting for you.
I sat there every morning
On the window sill
And thought of the very moment
When I would be there and reached the top,
Having achieved my goals too.
Yes, I wanted it and longed for that precise moment.
I could see it in my over imaginative mind's eye.
I prayed, fasted, cried, and still hoped I still had time.
And seeing all of it scared the hell out of me.
I was afraid of my own greatness.
I was a parent too, and I still am,
And looked at my kids too,
Hoping that they would not waste nine years of their lifetimes
On being too busy but ineffective.
I realised my parents' pain.

I felt my lower abdomen go cold at the thought of my children
    failing.
Turning into nothings, but full of gifts and talents.
I vowed from then on that, if not for myself too,
I would make my life count and my parents proud.
I finally opened that window to the possibilities.
And boy, is it rewarding!

The hunter, hunted

Every morning at dawn
Just as the moon made her bed and allowed day to start his
    shift,
Just as the morning fog hid itself in plain sight amidst the
    growing strength of light,
The neighbourhood would wake up to screams of terror.
A mother who'd stayed up all night worrying,
Hopeful that her son would enter through that door and say,
    "I'm safe".
Her prayers fell in the hands of a merciless killer, a hunter
Who only hunted at night. Never seen but always heard of.
He was the ruler of the nights
And he had devoured the son of this poor woman.
Wolves and beasts that roam all night long were afraid of him.
Witches and wizards never bothered him either.
He worked without any disturbances. He hunted souls freely.
Every night, he marked his register and he passed his
    assignment.
Wives were left widows because of this hunter.
Children were left orphans, and homes child-headed.
The township knew no peace because of this hunter.

Enough was enough!
The community had had enough deaths.
Enough screams, cries and sorrows caused by this beast.
Young men, old men, all left their homes on one particular
    night
To go look for the monster that ate their loved ones.
They stayed up all night, waiting, scared, worried and anxious.

Behold, a young man appeared with his weapons,
Ready to punish, ready to kill.
One more man, who was coming home from work,
Tired and trying to provide for his family.
The hunter, the young man, was ready to kill another man.
Because in his disturbed mind he had to rid this world of men
Because of all the pain that his father had caused him by
    beating him daily.
Because of the pain he'd caused him by killing his mother.
Because of the pain he'd caused to society by stealing, by
    raping and by killing.
That list was what the hunter told the young men and old men
    who caught him.
His anger caused him to paint all men with the same brush: a
    monster colour.
He thought that every man who walked the streets at night
    was up to no good.
He thought he was keeping the community safe, and so he
    wanted to kill them.
His pain drove him to do all that.
Instead of arresting him, or killing him, they healed him.
They hunted the hunter in him. They saved the young man and
    gave him love.
They showed him a side of a man that he never knew.
They cured his pain. They hunted the hunter.
The hunter was caught, and the community was safe again.

Expect me to call

Expect me to call.
I am sorry if I sound too protective.
It is okay if you suggest jealousy.
I do not care if he's having fun;
I care that he gets home safely.
So, expect me to call him
And ask if he has left already.
And if not, what could be holding him up?
Expect me to estimate the time
He should arrive home after he has left.
To get worried if he takes longer.
And heavens! Expect me to yell.
Expect me to yell at him for speeding
If he dares arrive too early
Because it was on a day like this,
A night like this actually,
Not far away from home,
When we nearly made it home, but a car appeared.
It was on a day like this
When everything went well
Except when it started to pour.
Yes, it was on a day like this –
Night rather, let me say –
When it was raining, and we were warm.
We were safe in our family car
That took us from a to b to z,
That took us to special days like today.
We were warm while watching the showers.
And bam!

Another car just appeared.
There was no way other than colliding.
We had to face the near-death experience.
We had been in an accident that nearly took our lives.
So, ever since then
I cannot relax when he's not home.
I cannot shake the fear
And I cannot silence the banging sound.
I pray that the Lord protects us.
That we never experience it again.
I am fearful,
But also I am faithful to the Lord.
So, I repeat:
Call me jealous or call me protective.
But for the love I have,
I am not ready for loss.
I am not ready for a lonely widow journey,
If there is such a word.
I will stay awake when he is away.
I will say that prayer and make that call.
Until he is safe with me,
Until the kids shout, Daddy! Daddy!
Until then, expect me to call.

I am jealous of your heart

I am jealous of the room.
One that has kept all the hurt but still shines through the
    windows.
One that knows all my secrets and still feels no need to tell.
One whose colours have been changed many times
But still maintains its original beauty.
One that chose and still chooses to remain rigid and firm.
I am jealous of the room that has seen through the door and its
    windows
Possibilities and opportunities to get better tenants,
But chose and still chooses to host my furniture and be firm.
I am jealous of the room that has suffered fights
But still waits for peace and reconciliation.
A room that has endured all seasons and heard all reasons.
A room that has endured all conditions and bared all
    situations
But still chose not to judge.
A room that withstood the pressure and temptations.
A room that hears songs and cries.
A room that sucked both blood and tears,
And water both clean and dirty,
But kept its form, nonetheless.
I am jealous of the room
Whose size has been criticised and its cracks mocked.
A room once compared to bigger and better and newly
    refurbished ones
But that still chose to be content and unshaken.

I am jealous of the room that in winds kept its warmth
And in heated situations never melted.
I am jealous of the room that knew its worth and kept it.
Such a room is your soul.
Such a room is your heart.

Yet to be

Yet to be.
A song yet to be composed.
A story yet to be written.
A poem yet to be recited.
I am a song yet to be composed.
My soul still travels around,
Listening to the beat my heart makes,
Echoing from the depth of my spiritual being
My connections to the people around me
And the vibrations they create as we interact.
I am the soprano that drags you out of your deep sleep
And the alto that calms your nerves
Just when you think you have left earth and entered the
    heavens.
I am the bass that sends peace to your troubled soul
As it gives a wake-up slap to the tenor that sends you to the
    holy shrine
To confess and ask pardon for your sins.
For I am a gospel of truth, undisputed and unshakable.

I am a song yet to be composed.
I am a story yet to be written.
My inspiration comes from the deep history of my people.
Their rich beliefs and their foundations of love;
Their songs of pride and praise to the giver of life.
My identity seeks no validation from the modern world that is
    lost to likes and followers.
I am a story rich with purity and rawness,

Untamed by the wild needs to be noticed in societal
    expectations of cool and dope.
I am a calabash of memories, traced and kept.
Footsteps marked and edged in the caves of old African history
    yet to be told.

I am a story yet to be written.
I am a poem yet to be recited.
Born and bred of the proud African sun
That gave rise to the kings and queens
Who came before me.
Their rhythm as they stomped the earth in dance
From songs created from the memories told by their stories.
I flow like the rivers and rhyme like sweet melodies of bird
    chirps
As they greet the good morning sun,
Waking up the nation's hopes for a better tomorrow.
I am the ancient tale our grandparents used to tell us around
    the fire.
A narration of their almost silent murmurs as they pray to the
    Lord
For my world to be a better place.
And, until I get there,
I am a song yet to be composed.
A story yet to be written.
A poem yet to be recited.
I am yet to be.

Like a potter's vessel

Like a potter's vessel
Caressed to utmost beauty,
I am a work of GOD'S hands.
My beauty lies not in the eyes of the mortals;
My beauty lies within the calm waters
Poured from a muddy vessel
That lay under big shade trees,
Blown by humble winds,
Refreshing to the soul and mind
And quenching a dreadful thirst.

Like a potter's vessel
I was carefully shaped and drawn.
Adorned with wonders of mercy.
I find myself all praiseworthy,
Not from the world
But from the inner, content me.
From a soul that echoes songs of praise
My life is a beautiful song
Whose lyrics rhyme beautifully in praise.
I am a work of GOD'S hands.
I am a fairy tale that knows no tragedy
For amid thunderstorms,
Like a potter's vessel,
I am hardened and made strong
Because in extreme heat from the sunshine
The calm waters inside give me peace.
Warm enough to soothe a new born baby,
Whose mother carefully bathes.

I am a work of GOD'S hands.
I find no errors in my creation
And therefore, the coming generation,
The coming congregation,
Shall sing a gospel of truth
And praise His name for my being.
Songs of praises shall raise on high.
His holy name shall reign.
His legacy, through me, shall prevail.
Forever and ever
It shall be.

QUOTES FOR YOU AND ME

Prayer for mercy

Prayer for mercy.
This time I am weak, my Lord.
Please forgive me and fill me up.
I cannot stop thinking of the worst, but I know You are the
  best.
You are true, forever and always.
Help us to find a way and not go astray.
We need you, Lord, to fill us up.
To replenish our faith and bestow in our hearts
Your peace and contentment
With utmost abundance.
This time I am weak, my Lord.
Please forgive me and fill me up.

A clean slate

A new day is another chance to start over.
Do not make the same mistake.
Lessons are hard, but the experience is worth it.
But focus. Not all trials make good inspiration.
Some are a waste of your fuel.
It is a long journey.
Safe travels.

Be still

It is okay to be silent.
For the loud obsession to be relevant,
To be seen, to be heard, to be there, to be noticed,
Is but a poison served in a golden glass.

My scars are not a curse

My scars are not a curse.
They tell a story of your lineage –
The kind you are proud to narrate.
You may see no more beauty in me
But hey, I am happy to be the author.
Scarred and weary as I am,
I am woman, I am king.

They are looking

They are looking.
I am prepared,
But very challenged internally and externally.
But it is not about me anymore. I have built a fan base
That I must keep entertained.
Literally and figuratively speaking,
I must dance to the different tunes.

Find your warrior

Focus.
Find your warrior.
Blurry eyes deprive clear vision.
Wipe away the tears, take a deep breath and soldier on.
That is where your true warrior is found:
Within yourself.

Be kind

My child, please be kind.
Before you ever become arrogant and boastful
Remember that there are people
For whom, no matter how hard and smart they work,
No matter how much effort they put in,
Things just never work out.
Be thankful, be considerate, and be kind.
Love, Mom

It was never your fault

It was not your fault.
It was not your fault that they could not hold themselves back.
We all have a choice.
We are all worth it.
You are all worth it.
Never let anyone make you feel otherwise.
Love and light...

Mother

A mother is more than just a woman, her womb, nine months
    of pregnancy, natural birth or C-section, sleepless nights,
    swollen breasts, and a tired body.
A mother is a source of life, wisdom and knowledge.
A mother is an extension of one's being.
Every little trait of strength and courage comes from her veins
And silver stripes edged on her pregnant body and she
    prepared you for life on earth.
She is a teacher and, if you listen well,
Dear daughter, dear son, you are already a master.

Father

A father should be as sweet as mine.
He is a hero. He is a provider.
A protector and a shield.
Just as they say, no bad deed goes unpunished,
No good deed goes unnoticed either.
We see you Dad, the intentional love, the care,
And the funny faces you make when you try not to blush.
We see you and we appreciate all that you are.
May you live long, because the world needs soldiers like you.

Thank you for the pictures

I long for you. I look at you every day and think of
How life would have been if you were still around.
I look at you and I am thankful for the day we decided
To take the picture that is so dear to me.
I look at you and I am thankful for all the memories
We have shared together, and I still feel your love.
I may no longer touch you, but with this picture I know
I will be able to see you forever, I know you are with me.
Thank you for the little stories you left us with.
Thank you for the pictures...

I'm thankful for your love

Being loved right is the most important feeling to ever
    experience.
Today, I woke up with so many emotions,
But the biggest of them all is gratitude and love.
Counting would be an injustice because I would forget some of
    the most important stuff,
The little things. The small ones that add up to the biggest
    picture.
Lord, I am thankful. My heart is content.
Not for the materials, but for your service to my joy,
My peace and my soul.
For your love, I am thankful.
I am thankful for your love.

Do not give up

To be able to crown oneself with achievement
Shows the greatest honour to self.
No matter how far away it looks,
It is always achievable.
Never give up.
Never give in.
Never grow weary.

LOVE LETTERS

This chapter of the book is written with appreciation to all our loved ones for the joy they bring to our hearts. I am thankful for the gift of life, the grace and mercy bestowed upon us, the opportunities to experience love in all its shapes and forms.

If there's someone you would love to show your love and gratitude to, then you're sure to find the right words in this book and, moreover, you are welcome to pick a few to share with them. From me, this book is dedicated to my parents, my husband, our kids, my siblings and to the strangers that I picked on the journey of life and made into my friends. We live in a world of happy pictures and broken souls. To be able to find someone worthy of love that they reciprocate is true wealth. We are poorer without love.

My mother

She woke up every morning to go to work,
Yet she made sure I ate in the morning.
That I had lunch at school and when I got home after school.
She put food on the table every night.
She kept me warm during windy days
And kept me dry in the rainy season.
She did everything in her capability
To put a smile on my face when I was sad.
She laughed with me when I felt like crying,
Took my pain when I was hurt.
When the world hated me, she loved me.
When my friends turned on me, she played with me.
She never read me a bedtime story before I slept –
I would be lying if I said she did –
But she knelt beside my tiny bed every night
And prayed to the Almighty God
To wake us up again the next morning
And bless our days as we soared on to a better future.
Mologadi did not buy me new clothes every month end.
But she knit out the hole at the back of my jeans,
Washed them with love
And made them new again.
The scent I still carry in my heart
And I wore them with pride of my mom's love.
She spelled with me when I could not read.
She held my small left hand with a smile,
And put the pen between my fingers,
And taught me how to write.
She nurtured me as I grew into the writer I am today.

Grown as I am, she still raises me from a distance.
I can never thank her enough.
She taught me peace, love, forgiveness.
And, most importantly, to give selflessly
Without expecting in return what I give.
She gave life, wisdom and a loving heart that never runs out.
For that, Mologadi is my queen.
For her, I am thankful.

My Father

I remember laughing so loud
When I met the old women who called me stupid
For looking so much like my father.
"She should have been a boy and swapped with her little
    brother,"
Said one of the three old women,
Who got offended by my laughing response and walked past.
My father gave me life.
Yes, he did not carry me like my mother did,
But he loved her with the big tummy and round shape.
He sang for me in the womb.
Hence, I took his voice and I recognised him when we first
    met.
I embraced his presence with a smile.
He gave me money for lunch at school,
And yet he walked many kilometres to work.
He came home very tired on such days,
And I would be telling a lie if I ever said I heard him
    complaining.
He always took it with a smile and said to us,
Fear not, for your futures are brighter than ours.
I will always cherish the storytelling nights
When, when there was no electricity.
Madimetja would gather us around him
And tell us old fairy-tale stories of the rabbit and the lion,
And the monkey and the jackal.
And, no matter how many times he repeated them,
With the voice he used they sounded new and even funnier.
Never has he laid a harsh hand on me,

Nor has he ever threatened my life if I wronged him.
He led a charismatic life as a father, husband and friend to his
    family,
So good that I pictured a suitor like him.
I learned what love is and should be from him.
I am happy that the Lord chose him for us,
To have him as our father
Never mind those who called me stupid
For looking like Madimetja.
They are merely reminding me of my fortunes,
Praising my biggest blessing:
To be like him, to be of his offspring.
I am the daughter of a hero, my hero.
I am my father's daughter with pride.

The butterflies have come

The butterflies have come.
It is January again
And the butterflies came.
But this time I could not call you to boast.
I could not dance provocatively and say I saw them first.
While this hurt, it also made me realise
That from now on everything begins without you.
Heaven could not wait, but I get it, Mama.
I get it, Mama, don't you worry.

I know and I saw how painful it was for you.
I saw your body was weary
And I saw how your soul needed its rest.
I know it was selfish of me, of us,
To expect you to hold on
When not even one of us was able
To carry your pain just for an hour.
But it is well, Mama; you are gone now.
I hope you have healed.

I hope you have forgiven and forgotten
The ills of this world.
I hope your scars have healed and been wiped away.
And I hope you still smile.
I know I will never touch you again,
But I know you have not left me.
I have never been ready to say it.
But I powerlessly write on this paper now:
Rest in peace, my dearest mom.

All my life my biggest fear was of losing you.
At times I feel like I am suffocating.
I constantly run to my phone to call you
And my heart shatters each time I realise that calling you
Can only be in prayer and lamentation.
But may your soul finally get its needed rest.
May your soul find its home in God's guarded heaven.
And, when it has finally quenched its thirst for rested peace,
May you, together with the other angels, remember us.
May you guard over us and our children,
Protect us and guide us, Mologadi.
But for now, my queen,
Get your needed sleep and rest in peace.

My African queen

My eyes into her eyes
Dip into her soul.
My African queen.
Her beauty drips of wonder.
She walks like thunder.
She makes my world tremble
And brings me to my knees.
Her smile calms my spirit.
She shuts out all the other noises at the sound of her melody.
She speaks wisdom and sings a harmony.
Oh, my African queen.
From her, flows the stream of life.
From the trims of her silver linings, I see only beauty.
Might I please be the beast, but one that loves?
So that we can be the beauty and the beast?
She is truly a Godly masterpiece.
She needs no throne for her royal highness,
For wherever she sits, marks of royalty are edged for life
And generations to come shall tell her tales and sing her
    praises.
Oh, my African queen.

My Children

To my children:
How do I find the words?
How do I describe this love?
You have taught me so much about myself
That I did not know was there.
You stretch my love in a manner I never thought possible.
You taught me how each emotion can go an extra mile.
Love, care, happiness, anger and patience.
These five you have overly stretched over the years.
You have taught me balance.
When I thought I would struggle to love you all the same,
Like a puzzle, you taught me that
I cannot have this one without the other...
To have the complete picture.
Each one with its own shape
Adds its own chapter to the whole story.
As a mother, I have been rebooted over and over.
When I thought I'd had enough
Your smile healed me.
Your vulnerability woke my strength up
To carry fiercely the cross on my shoulders for
Just one more day, each day.
Your laughter reminded me
Just how beautiful the world is.
Your endless calling and screaming reminded me
Just how Mom is the most beautiful name in the world.
The tears in my eyes remind me daily that
I may never get my youth back.
Your love reminds me that

I can never be completely alive and accomplished without you.
You are a part of God's mission to create life through me.
You are my world.
All of you...
I love you, I love you, I love you.

My Husband

To my husband:
You changed me from a little girl to a woman.
You loved me dearly.
You became an answered prayer.
You showed me what a good husband is.
You showed my parents that they can trust you with their
    princess' life.
You created a safe space for my heart.
You created a trust in me.
You became my best friend, my world;
You became my soulmate.
When I came across pain and predicament,
You held me and healed me.
When you came across pain and predicament,
You allowed me to hold you and heal you.
My world can never be the same without you.
I pray that we will always love each other.
I pray that we will be each other's forever.
I pray that I will be your peace, as you will be mine.
I pray that you find happiness in the days of our love and lives.
I hurt, just by thinking of losing your love and affection.
I hurt, just by thinking of our ending – God forbid.
I am thankful for the kind of husband you are.
I am thankful for your companionship.
I love you. I love loving you. I love having you.

Remember to smile

Remember to smile.
Open me when days are dark,
So that I can be your light.
Open me when you feel alone,
So that I can remind you that I will always be here.
Open me when you feel weak,
So that I can tell you that you are my strength.
Open me when you are weary,
So that I can replenish you with love.
Open me when you feel like you are not enough,
So that I can remind you we are incomplete without you.
Open me when you feel invisible,
So that I can touch you wherever you hide.
Open me when you want to cry,
So that I can give you tears of joy.
Open me when you feel small,
So that I can show you what a giant you are.
Open me when you feel less loved,
So that I can show you how you stretch my love the extra mile.
Open me when you feel defeated,
So that I can remind you what a warrior you are.
Open me when you feel your wings are broken,
So that I can fly high with you and soar.
Open me when you wake up every morning,
So that I can remind you to smile.

Woman of Worth

Woman of worth,
Oh, you beautiful mother of the nation!
So beautiful, with big black eyes
Adorning your big, rounded, sun-kissed black face.
As black as dark chocolate
Shining under the proud African sun,
You carry the world on your wide shoulders
As you proudly walk tall in your rich and virgin beauty.
You adorn your body with beads and wrap it with nature's
    printed cloths.
You walk proud as a cat, tail up high,
As your voluptuous thighs and bums hit the sides
In tune, as you step left and right,
With your thick feet stomping the ground.
Your walk is as mighty as the lion
That knows it is the king of the jungle.
You are a treasured work of God's hands.
You are a woman of worth.
You are a treasured possession that
Men of this world lust to have but cannot own.
You are unique, with your big nose that breathes love,
Your fat lips that are lusted for and sought after,
For what comes out of them are words filled with wisdom.
You are no ordinary woman
For where you have passed marks of beauty and wisdom are
    edged.

Pride and praise live within the hearts of those who have you,
Those who thank God for you, every day.
Because you are a woman of worth.
You are a work of God's hands.
Woman, you are worthy, and I cannot ever praise you enough.

Makaziwe!

Makaziwe... Let her be known that
She is the story of many tears unseen.
A story of many screams and cries unheard.
She is a book of many tales untold and many songs unsung.
She is a pot of emotions ignored, aspirations denied, and
    dreams crushed.
She is a trunk of riches and treasures undiscovered.
She is a river made of bloodshed from periods and punches.
She is a combination of many women toiled with, lied to and
    treated the same.
Shamed, battered, bruised, crushed, cut, thrown away and
    discarded.
Let it be known... that she is no waste
Let it be known... that she is no trash.
Let her be known... Makaziwe.
She is beauty hidden in chores and childbirth and body
    shaming.
She is leadership hidden in submission and respect for the
    mighty man.
She is royalty hidden in traditions and protocols.
She is knowledge hidden under dirty slumps in the hood.
She is the forbidden fruit in the garden of success.
She is the unqualified in the room of decisions made on her
    behalf about her life.
She is an object of sexual satisfactions and fantasies of the
    man.
She is the truth unspoken for fear of dishonour and disrespect.

She is weakness dressed in the size of her fists compared to
    her opponent.
Or rather, her oppressor, the man of her dreams.
OKAY, THAT'S NONSENSE! LET ME REDEFINE HER
LET HER BE KNOWN... MAKAZIWE!
She is a force to be reckoned with.
A masterpiece to admire.
A fire one cannot extinguish and ice one cannot melt.
She is a gentle storm brewing in the atmosphere.
Dare not to trample on her emotions or face the storm!
She is a mystery none can solve,
A discovery yet to be made.
She is all the love and all the peace in the world.
A thirst never to be quenched.
Let it be known... no one can define her!
Let it be known... no one can cage her!
Let her be known... Makaziwe!
She is power.
She is leadership.
She is amazing and astonishing.
She is a success story, and she is unstoppable.
She is capable and undeniably strong.
She is wisdom and warmth dressed in her ability to nurture.
She is clothed with care and unimaginable empathy.
She thrives in even the hardest of hardships.
She wins, even in the toughest of challenges.
She loves, even when charged with hate.
She forgives, even when showered with pain.
It is within her.
It is her superpower.
It is her greatest strength.

It is time you know her... Makaziwe.
It is time!
You will know her.
You will see her, and you will hear her.
You will embrace her, and you will acknowledge her.
You will seek her, and you will find her.
Mighty and worthy,
Powerful and passionate,
Beautiful and charismatic,
Able and capable!
Ever strong and ever ready.
Its time! You will know her.!
Let her be known... Makaziwe!
Let her be known... Makaziwe!
Let her be known... Makaziwe!

I WILL FIND YOU

I will find you.
I write this letter to you,
Knowing very well how hurt you are.
I realise that you had the worst experience of me,
Personified by ruthless, selfish beings,
Only ever looking out for their own needs.
I know about the sleepless nights:
The endless hospital visits;
The broken ribs and the torn apart heart;
The torn soul and the faded hope for change.
I am sorry you endured all that.
Allow me to make a new promise to you
That, be it today, tomorrow or next year, I will find you.
Allow me to extend my deepest apologies to you
And say that it was not me
Because when my time comes you will feel the difference.
I beg you not to look at the time on your wristwatch,
Not the time and date on the calendar on your wall,
But to prepare and make space for me because I'm close to
    finding you.
I can already feel the vibrations of your soul nearby.
I hear the echoes of your pain, distrust and doubt.
I will mend your ribs, and your heart, and your soul, and your
    hope.
I will return your sleepless nights to peaceful ones
And I know that right now I am asking a lot from you

Because those who hurt you also came like me but, fortunately
    for me,
I am invisible. I am an open book.
And my promise is that, wanting or not, accepting or not, I will
    find you.
And when I finally do, I will stay forever.
Yours truly, Love.

www.ingramcontent.com/pod-product-compliance
Lightning Source LLC
Chambersburg PA
CBHW031326060726
47590CB00003B/1344